3 AM Thoughts

Anna Ridgeway

3 AM THOUGHTS

CONTENTS

Hi there, I'm glad you found me. This book first and foremost is meant to make you feel heard. To make you realize that you are not the only one feeling these emotions. 3 AM Thoughts is mean to explain the indescribable--the never ending what ifs that circulate through your head when you are supposed to be sleeping. It will all work out--I promise you that. I love you!
-anna

I

DUSK

HEARTBREAK

You know the feeling
That suckerpunch to your gut
That takes the breath right out of you
It's one of the worst types of pain
invisible,
mean,
and long lasting

Heartbreak knows no age limit
He hurts at 15 crying in your childhood bed-
room
Hurts at 21 when they choose her over you
And hurts just as bad at 24

When you realize he wasn't the one

Heartbreak is a manmade thing
The perfect mix of guilt, pain, and anger
Built for our destruction

And yet
We put ourselves through it
Time and time again
For the chance
For the possibility
Of love

You deserve better:

You deserve better
Says my best friend
And my mom
His friends too

He's not worth your energy
Says my sister
My dad
My therapist too

How do I explain

To each and every one of you
That those lines
Well meaning as they may be
Don't. Mean. shit.

Because when I look in the mirror
Trying to recognize myself
Who I've become
You know what I say to myself?

You deserve him
You deserve to get to laugh with him
Talk to him
Love him

Oh and my energy?
Worthless without him right there next to me
At my very side

So I not along politely
Pretending to agree
Knowing perfectly well
That nothing you could say
Would make me not want him

Because the truth is
I lot myself believe
That this could be it

This was my time
To be happy
To be comforted
To be loved

So if you don't mind
I'd like you and your judgement
To go far away
And I can go back to my daydream
Of him still here with me

A dream where he didn't give up
A dream where he didn't walk away
A dream of us
The way we used to be

Overwhelm

It's not a math problem
It can't be solved
I can't make the numbers fit

Just give me a multiplication problem
Or even some long division
Carry the one
Don't forget your decimal place
It's satisfying

Clear
Predictable

So then why can't I figure it out
This stupid problem
There has to be a right answer
Just has to be

But until then that time
That lightbulb moment
It just sits
Stagnant in my brain
Forever

I don't wanna know

It's human nature to ask questions
I get that
Everyone wants an explanation
The why behind what happens to them
But sometimes
It's better not to know

If I asked him why we ended
Why he gave up on me
Why he left
Who knows what he would say

I'm sure he would have some excuse
I was too much
Or not enough
Whatever the answer
It would make me feel like I was inadequate
I needed to change
And I don't
I won't

So as much as I'd love to know
Why he did what he did
I think I'm better
Staying in the unknown

Growing up:

You are 21
You live in an apartment
That never smells quite right
With its overflowing trash cans
That never really empty
That stain that never came off the counter
No matter how hard you scrubbed
You're in a fight with your roomates
About who drank that last beer in the fridge
You're stressed

Because you slept through your 9 am
After binging Friends last night
You are 21

Suddenly you are 22
Your roommate accepted a nursing job
She'll be moving out in a month
Your boyfriend got in to Med School
He's busy writing essays
Finishing his clinical apps
Your well meaning aunt asks you at Thanksgiv-
ing
What will you be doing next year?
Where will you live?
Who will you live with?

It's only a year apart
I look the same
Act the same
Yet society is telling you two completely differ-
ent things
So now I'm 22
But all I am really wanting
Is to stay at 21

What's a spark?

Is it a candle in a dark room
A quiet light
That gives you peace?

Is it a spotlight
On a huge stage
That follows you
Every way you turn?

Or a sun
Thats so bright you can physically feel the af-
fects
Almost too bright
Blinding when you look at it?

I wonder
I sit in my dark space
And I wonder

The people pleaser:

Yes!
I say
A bright smile on my face
I'd love to!

I say
My voice raises an octave
Sounds great!
I say
Eyes slowly looking around

Why is it so hard for me to say yes to myself
When I spend all my time saying yes
To my friends
To my boyfriend
Even to my family
Why is it

I'm so scared to see them hurt
but in the meantime
I'm hurting myself

The difference

The kid I babysit
Asked me what type of person I want to marry
With the innocence
That only a child possesses
I gave her a vague answer
Not ready to let my mind go down that road
But that night
As I was drifting off to sleep

The question continued to swirl in my thoughts

He'll have your confidence
Your love of life
Your love of people
Perfectly contrasting with my fear of them

I hope he has your enthusiasm
Continually pushing me to try new things
I hope he treats me like how you did
Putting me first
Time and time again

There's a lot
That you, my first love
Will share
With him, my last love
But the difference?

He'll stay
He'll keep his promises
He won't walk away
So despise what y'all will share
That's what will make the difference

Between the man I thought I would marry
And the man I will

II

3 AM

. I have this thing
A problem I guess you could call it
If I'm really being honest

You see, my brain thinks night is it's playground
To second guess
To wonder
To stress

And when you're 20
And on that weird brink
Teetering on the edge
Of childhood and adulthood
3 am is scary
Am I following my passion
Am I supposed to be meeting the love of my life
Or worse did I already

Am I happy?
Am I content?

Ask me in the morning I say
I'll complete my to do list
Happy and cheery to the outside eye
But damn
It's the 3 am I'm scared of
When my true feelings come out
And I'm powerless to stop them
Powerless and confused
3 am

Resilience

How could you?
You looked me in the eyes
And told me you feel nothing
Looked me in the eyes
And told me it was all a mistake

Wow
I thought I was strong
I thought I was tough
But not for you.
Not for that.

I thought you destroyed me
Broke me into too many pieces
It would be impossible to glue back together

But you know what?
I think I'm more resilient then you gave me
credit for
Because I'm still here
By myself

Still moving
Somehow
Everyday
Still moving

Since you

I parallel parked for the first time in years
Learned how to make eggs
Just like you always did for me
Found a new favorite song
That I never listened to with you

I learned how to stand up for myself
Without you to fight my battles for me
I did a quick switch
From passenger princess to driver

I cried my heart out
Had panic attacks
Without you to comfort me

But also,

I found a few butterflies
That weren't for you
Thought about my future
With no place for you
Did new things
Without you to convince me
Loved myself
Even though you didn't

Honestly?

I survived
Without you
And that's something to be proud of

The Voice:

You know that little voice
The inner critic who reminds you
Of that cellulite on your leg
Or weird noise you make when you laugh

Determined to drag you down
Hurt your confidence
Well for me,
That inner voice
Is you

Your voice is deeper than mine
Raspier
With a hint of edge to it
It knows my weaknesses
Maybe even better then I do
Knows that one spot

For me,
My "achilles heel"
Is you

The future:

Sometimes I think about the future
I think about mine a lot
But that scares me
So then I think about yours

How weird those are two separate things
Not our future
My future
And your future
Completely unrelated
Connected only by some memory
Long in the past

Do you still want it
That future you planned with me?
Is everything the same
Just with me no longer there
No longer the one by your side?

You promised me the future
You promised me a lot of things
But it turns out

I loved a liar
Or at least you became one
I loved someone cruel
Or at least you acted that way
I loved a stranger
Or at least that's who you became

I can imagine a lot of your future
Except for one detail
I can't imagine the one by your side

I can't imagine the one who's not me
Turns out even my imagination has it's limits

Time:

Sometimes I think time is your best friend
Because truthfully
I pity whoever is by your side
Whoever has to deal with the way you approach
life
The carelessness
The selfishness
Once I admired this about you
So impressed by someone who could make a de-
cision
Without overthinking every possible outcome
But I've discovered

Anxiety is not the weakness I made it to be
Anxiety is not the weakness you made it to be

Anxiety is the willingness to express your emo-
tions
Even If it scares you
It is a strength

A maturity
That you never had

Thinking about you
Honestly makes me laugh
Because whether you are the happiest person
alive
Or the saddest
I no longer care
Because I don't want to be in it

Comparison:

For so long
When I look in the mirror
I saw me
Yes
But I saw you too

Decades of quotes replay in my memory
She's taller
My grandma says
She's more talkative
My older sister says
She's skinnier
The boyfriend says
I can't explain to you how long it took

For me to look at myself
As a separate entity from her
For me to look at myself
Without comparing to her

And the worst part?
She's my best friend
I love her energy
Her enthusiasm
Her looks
I want to be her number one supporter

But secretly
From a dark deep place of myself
That I didn't know existed

I compare
Everything
I compare
Our moods
Our looks
Our friends

And sometimes I think about
How the universe convinced me
To go through life
me vs her
Instead of

us vs them
And that
Is something I'll never forgive it for

The distraction

Sometimes I wish it was you
Those times late at night
When my bed is feeling just a little too big
When the urge to reread my texts
Feels just a little too strong
I know you would want it
I know it would be easy
So why is it not enough

Maybe that's my sign
I'm not strong enough
For now
I guess I'll just sit here
Reflecting
Analyzing
Guessing
What my future my holds
Who my future holds

III

DAWN

AUTONOMY:

. I've always believed
I have control over my own life
My own destiny
My feelings
And I want you to know
You do too

You wake up in the morning
It's a brand new day
Might as well make it great
You could save a stranger's life today
Meet your bestfriend
Your future husband

Or both

Today is full of opportunity
If you would just see the blue sky
Instead of getting distracted in the clouds

My biggest lesson:

Trust me
I know first hand
I know how easy it is
To find someone
You really enjoy
To find someone
And let them break down all your walls
Let them know you
Let them have you

But trust me
No matter what they say
How much they care
You have to keep boundaries

And no it's not to keep the hurt out
Like I used to think
Not to block him out
But I have learned

If any relationship is going to work
With a friend
Or a spouse
They can't be your everything

I mean, come on
Why would you want one person
To control that much of you
It's not a matter of trust
Or lack of it
It's a matter of self love

I should always value myself most
Not someone else
No matter what
And I never realized
Until you
How much I would value
You not valuing me

No, that's not fair
Fine
I value that I'm not your only priority
That I'm not the only aspect of your life
That could make you happy

There's you
And there's me

And there's us
But it's not just an "us"
And thats what matters

How did you do it:

What's your secret?
You speak
And I trust you
I look at you
And I want to tell you everything about me
You talk about the future
And I agree
100%

I don't know if I should be scared
Or excited
That you take away my logic
You take away the promise I made to myself
That I wouldn't make myself vulnerable
That I wouldn't let myself be hurt again
That it wasn't worth it

But suddenly?
It is worth it

It's not a logical decision

Not one I consciously make
It's just a feeling
A comfort
A butterfly
Or two or three
That makes me want to talk to you
Need to talk to you
At all times

Somehow,
A year of pain
Didn't matter so much
Suddenly,
The chance of you
Is worth it
Worth the pain
Worth the hurt
Worth the numbness
And maybe I'll live to regret this decision
But somehow
The decision is already out of my hands

Your choice

You have made your choice
Loud and clear
So now I'm making mine

I don't care when it is
When you realize what you lost
If it's a few months
Or years
It will be too late.

I appreciate you
The time you gave me
The love
The standards
I will always remember them

But finally
It's time
I'm making my choice

My hope:

My friends would tell you
I'm full of hope
Full of what could be
Hope for the future
And that's true yes
I'll always root for love
For friendship
For happiness
It's not in my nature

To root for anything else

But I'll be honest
Once in a while I wonder
If hope gets me in more trouble than it's worth
Would I be less hurt
If I didn't see the good
The possibilities
In everything
In Everyone?

But when I think about it,
Why would I purposefully go through a life with
no color
Why would I purposefully exclude the pink
The purple
The blue
Because as much as hope hurts me
No matter how many tears I shed
I refuse to live in a life with no hope
A life with no color
A life of black and white

Strangers!

There's a lot of bad in the world

We all know this
The second we turn on the news
There's always something

But today
I wanted to talk about the good things
The small moments
The humanity

When you realize strangers are people too
When every car on the highway stops to let a cat
cross the road
Everyone taking a break
From their busy scheduled day
To save a life
Of something else

When every car stops for the ambulance
whizzing by
Recognizing that
No matter how bad their day
There's someone else who is having a worse one

When you see a dog pass you on the street
And you can't help but slow down
Can't help but talk to the dog
smile up at the owner
Bonding

For a split second
Over a shared feeling
Of love

When you see a baby in the grocery store
And smile at her instantly
Feeling your day brighten
By the innocence
Of someone so young

When you see someone lose their first love
And all you feel is empathy
And a blast to the past
Of scream crying in your bed
So many years ago
Over "the one"

There's a lot of bad in the world
Yes
But there's also good
The little things
That remind us
We are all connected

We are intertwined

Hi! My name is Anna Cook and I just graduated from Clemson University. I feel a lot of emotions-always have--always will. I'm much better at writing my emotions then explaining them so, I started to write when I was feeling particularly upset or sad. It turns out, once I started I couldn't quite stop. Publishing 3 AM Thoughts has been a dream of mine for as a long as I can remember. It helped me heal, and I hope it helps you too.